SUPER EASY
BURGERS

69 REALLY SIMPLE RECIPES

ORATHAY SOUKSISAVANH

PHOTOGRAPHS BY CHARLOTTE LASCÈVE

CLARKSON POTTER/PUBLISHERS
NEW YORK

Contents

american style

Burger with Fried Onions and Pickles ... 5

Cheeseburger ... 7

Double Cheeseburger ... 9

Bacon Cheeseburger ... 11

Cheese-Stuffed Burger ... 13

Pizza Burger ... 15

Spicy Cheesesteak ... 17

Pulled Pork and Red Cabbage ... 19

Onion Ring Burger ... 21

Chicken Nugget Burger ... 23

Chicken BLT ... 25

Chicken Caesar Burger ... 27

Hot Dog Burger ... 29

fren'cheese

Cantal and Shallot Burger ... 31

Beaufort and Mushroom Burger ... 33

Spinach and Blue Cheese Burger ... 35

Raclette Burger ... 37

Tartiflette Burger ... 39

Mont d'Or and Sausage Burger ... 41

Tomme and Rösti Burger ... 43

Apple Camembert Burger ... 45

Maroilles and Endive Burger ... 47

Muenster and Sauerkraut Burger ... 49

Mustard Beaufort Burger ... 51

Peppery Tomme and Chicken Burger ... 53

Laughing Cow and Ham Burger ... 55

around the world

Chicken Tikka Burger ... 57

Thai Curry Chicken Burger ... 59

Banh Mi Burger ... 61

Hawaiian Burger ... 63

Teriyaki Beef Burger ... 65

Yakitori Chicken Burger ... 67

Tonkatsu Burger ... 69

Tex-Mex Burger ... 71

Pineapple Mango Chicken Burger ... 73

Kofta Burger ... 75

Pesto Caprese Burger ... 77

Sun-Dried Tomato Chicken Burger ... 79

Mint Feta Chicken Burger ... 81

English Fry-Up Burger ... 83

Surf and Turf Burger ... 85

from the sea

Salmon Bagel 87

Tzatziki Dill Salmon Burger 89

Avocado Salmon Burger 91

Fish and Chips Burger.................... 93

Tartar Fried Fish Burger.................. 95

Bacalao and Piquillo Burger 97

Mayo Tuna Burger 99

Shrimp Meze Burger 101

Fried Calamari Burger with Aioli 103

Chorizo Cod Burger....................... 105

veggie

Pesto Grilled Veggies.................... 107

Eggplant Parm Burger 109

Mushroom Spinach Burger............. 111

Hummus Beet Burger 113

Veggie Pesto Caprese Burger.......... 115

Tzatziki Chickpea Burger................ 117

Gouda Navy Bean Burger.............. 119

Sweet Potato Burger 121

Piccalilli Veggie Burger 123

Guacamole Lentil Burger 125

Zucchini Frittata Burger.................. 127

Falafel Burger 129

Spanish Tortilla Burger................... 131

Soy Tofu Burger............................ 133

gourmet feast

Foie Gras Burger........................... 135

Parmesan Duck Burger.................. 137

Foie Gras and Duck Burger............ 139

Honey Mustard Duck Confit
    Burger..................................... 141

BURGER WITH FRIED ONIONS AND PICKLES

 10 minutes prep time

 5 minutes cooking time

 Serves 2

hamburger buns
x 2 large

hamburger patties
x 2 (⅓ pound)

pickle slices
to taste

ketchup
2 tablespoons

French-fried onions
2 tablespoons

mustard
2 tablespoons

○ Preheat oven to 350°F. Slice the buns in half, if necessary.

○ Heat oil in a pan. Season the patties with salt and pepper. Warm the buns in the oven for 5 minutes.

○ Cook the patties over high heat 1–2 minutes on each side. Spread the ketchup and mustard on the buns, then layer the patties, pickles, and French-fried onions. Top to finish.

CHEESEBURGER

 10 minutes prep time

 5 minutes cooking time

 Serves 2

hamburger buns
x 2 small

hamburger patties
x 2 (¼ pound)

pickle slices
to taste

onion
x ½ small

cheddar cheese
x 2 slices

ketchup
4 tablespoons

○ Preheat oven to 350°F. Cut the onion into thin round slices and slice the hamburger buns in half, if necessary.

○ Season the patties with salt and pepper. Warm the buns in the oven for 3 minutes.

○ Heat oil in a pan, then cook the patties over high heat 1–2 minutes on each side.

○ Spread the ketchup on the buns. Then place the patties and cheese slices on the buns. Melt in the oven for 2 minutes. Remove from the oven and add the pickles and onion slices, then top to finish.

american style

DOUBLE CHEESEBURGER

 10 minutes prep time

 5 minutes cooking time

 Serves 2

hamburger buns
x 2 large

hamburger patties
x 4 (⅙ pound)

pickle slices
to taste

yellow cheddar cheese
x 4 slices

white cheddar cheese
x 4 slices

ketchup
4 tablespoons

○ Preheat oven to 350°F. Slice the buns in half, if necessary.

○ Season the patties with salt and pepper. Warm the buns in the oven for 3 minutes.

○ Heat oil in a pan, then cook the patties over high heat for 30 seconds on each side. Place a piece of each kind of cheddar on each patty.

○ Spread the ketchup on the buns, place two patties with cheese on each bottom bun, and melt in the oven for 2 minutes. Add the pickles, then top to finish.

american style

BACON CHEESEBURGER

 15 minutes prep time

 35 minutes cooking time

 Serves 2

hamburger buns
x 2 large

hamburger patties
x 2 (⅓ pound)

onions
x 2 medium

cheddar cheese
x 2 slices

bacon
x 6 slices

barbecue sauce
4 tablespoons

○ Chop the onions, then sauté them in a pan over medium heat. Once lightly browned, lower the heat, add salt and pepper, and let caramelize for 20 minutes.

○ Preheat oven to 350°F. Cook the bacon in the oven for 12 minutes. Slice the buns in half, if necessary, and warm in the oven for 5 minutes.

○ Heat oil in a pan, then cook the patties over high heat 1–2 minutes on each side. Place a slice of cheddar on each patty and melt in the oven for 2 minutes.

○ Spread the barbecue sauce and caramelized onions on the buns, then place the patties on them and add 3 slices of bacon to each. Top to finish.

american style
CHEESE-STUFFED BURGER

🔪 **15 minutes prep time**

🍲 **5 minutes cooking time**

☺ **Serves 2**

hamburger buns
x 2 large

hamburger patties
x 2 (⅓ pound)

cheddar cheese
x 2 slices

red onion
x ½ medium

○ Preheat oven to 350°F. Cut the tomato and onion into thin round slices, and slice the buns in half, if necessary. Fold the cheese into cubes, then stuff one cube into each patty, sealing the sides well.

○ Season the patties with salt and pepper. Warm the buns in the oven for 5 minutes.

○ Heat oil in a pan and cook the patties over high heat for 1 minute on each side. Then heat in the oven 5–6 minutes.

○ Spread the special sauce on the buns, then arrange the tomato slices, patties, and onions. Top to finish.

tomato
x 1 medium

special sauce
4 tablespoons

american style

PIZZA BURGER

 10 minutes prep time

 7 minutes cooking time

 Serves 2

hamburger buns
x 2 large

hamburger patties
x 2 (⅓ pound)

mozzarella cheese
5 ounces

pepperoni
x 16 thin slices

tomato sauce
4 tablespoons

fresh basil
x 12 leaves

○ Preheat oven to 400°F. Thinly slice the cheese and cut the buns in half, if necessary.

○ Spread the tomato sauce on both sides of the buns, then top with cheese and pepperoni. Warm in the oven 5–7 minutes. Do not overcook the cheese.

○ Heat oil in a pan. Season the patties with salt and pepper, then cook over high heat for 2 minutes on each side. Arrange the basil leaves on the buns, then place the patties and top to finish.

SPICY CHEESESTEAK

 10 minutes prep time

15 minutes cooking time

Serves 2

hamburger buns
x 2 large

steak
½ pound

cheddar cheese
x 4 slices

onion
x 1 medium

jalapeño
x 1

garlic
x 1 clove

O Preheat oven to 350°F. Crush the garlic, chop the onion and jalapeño, and cut the steak into strips. Mix salt, pepper, and the crushed garlic and rub over the strips of steak. Cut the cheese into pieces and slice the buns in half, if necessary.

O Warm the buns in the oven for 5 minutes.

O Heat oil in a pan and caramelize the onion. Set aside. Sauté the steak over high heat for 1 minute, stirring. Add the onion, jalapeño, and cheese. Once the cheese melts, spoon the mixture onto the buns. Top to finish.

PULLED PORK AND RED CABBAGE

 15 minutes prep time

 1½ hours cooking time

 Serves 4

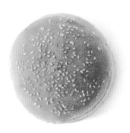

hamburger buns
x 4 large

pork loin
1 pound

○ Preheat oven to 400°F.

○ Rub salt and pepper on the pork loin, then place it in an oiled stockpot. Cover with water. Quarter the onions and add them to the pot. Bring to a boil, then cook in the oven, covered, for 1 hour and 15 minutes. Remove the loin, then let the cooking juices reduce on the stove for 10 minutes.

onions
x 2 large

carrots
x 2 large

○ Shred the carrots and chop the cabbage. Slice the buns in half, if necessary, and warm in the oven for 5 minutes at 350°F.

○ Shred the pork, then add the cooking juices and barbecue sauce. Serve the pork and vegetables in the buns.

red cabbage
several pieces

barbecue sauce
8 tablespoons

ONION RING BURGER

 10 minutes prep time

 20 minutes cooking time

 Serves 2

hamburger buns
x 2 large

hamburger patties
x 2 (⅓ pound)

onion rings
x 10 (packaged)

tomato
x 1 large

○ Cut the tomato into slices and slice the buns in half, if necessary.

○ Heat up the onion rings in the oven according to the instructions on the package. Place the buns in the oven for 5 minutes before taking out the onion rings.

○ Season the patties with salt and pepper. Heat oil in a pan and cook the patties over high heat, about 2 minutes on each side.

○ Spread the barbecue sauce on the buns. Arrange the tomato slices, lettuce, patties, and onion rings on the buns, then drizzle with more barbecue sauce. Top to finish.

butter lettuce
x 4 leaves

barbecue sauce
6 tablespoons

CHICKEN NUGGET BURGER

 5 minutes prep time

15 minutes cooking time

Serves 2

hamburger buns
x 2 large

chicken nuggets
x 6–8 (packaged)

tomatoes
x 2 small

iceberg lettuce
¼ head

mayonnaise
4 tablespoons

barbecue sauce
4 tablespoons

O Slice the tomatoes and cut the buns in half, if necessary. Chop the lettuce.

O Heat up the chicken nuggets in the oven according to the instructions on the package. Place the buns in the oven for 5 minutes before taking out the nuggets.

O Spread the mayonnaise on one side of the buns and barbecue sauce on the other. Arrange the tomatoes, nuggets, and lettuce on the buns, then top to finish.

CHICKEN BLT

 5 minutes prep time

 15 minutes cooking time

 Serves 2

hamburger buns
x 2 large

breaded chicken cutlets
x 2 (packaged)

tomatoes
x 2 small

bacon
x 6 slices

mayonnaise
4 tablespoons

romaine lettuce
x 8 leaves (hearts)

○ Cut the tomatoes into slices and slice the buns in half, if necessary.

○ Cook the bacon in the oven for 12 minutes at 350°F.

○ Heat up the chicken cutlets in the oven according to the instructions on the package. Place the buns in the oven for 5 minutes before taking out the chicken.

○ Spread the mayonnaise on the buns. Arrange the tomatoes, cutlets, bacon, and lettuce on the buns, then top to finish.

CHICKEN CAESAR BURGER

 15 minutes prep time

 5 minutes cooking time

 Serves 2

hamburger buns
x 2 large

chicken breasts
x 2 (⅓ pound)

○ Preheat oven to 350°F. Finely chop the chicken. Add salt and pepper, then shape into patties. Use a cheese slicer to shave off pieces of Parmesan.

romaine lettuce
x 8 leaves

aioli
4 tablespoons

○ Slice the buns in half, if necessary, and warm in the oven for 5 minutes.

○ Heat oil in a pan and cook the patties over medium heat 3–4 minutes on each side.

○ Spread the aioli on the buns, then layer the patties, anchovies, Parmesan, and lettuce. Top to finish.

oil-packed anchovies
x 6

Parmesan cheese
2 ounces

american style

HOT DOG BURGER

 5 minutes prep time

 15 minutes cooking time

 Serves 2

hamburger buns
x 2 large

hamburger patties
x 2 (¼ pound)

hot dogs
x 2

French-fried onions
2 tablespoons

ketchup
4 tablespoons

mustard
2 tablespoons

O Preheat oven to 350°F. Cut the hot dogs in half both crosswise and lengthwise.

O Slice the buns in half, if necessary, and warm in the oven for 5 minutes. Heat oil in a pan and brown the hot dogs 2–3 minutes.

O Season the patties with salt and pepper. Heat oil in a pan and cook over high heat 2–3 minutes on each side.

O Spread the ketchup and mustard on the buns, then arrange the patties, hot dogs, and French-fried onions. Top to finish.

CANTAL AND SHALLOT BURGER

 15 minutes prep time

 5 minutes cooking time

 Serves 2

hamburger buns
x 2 large

hamburger patties
x 2 (⅓ pound)

shallots
x 3

sherry vinegar
2 tablespoons

Cantal cheese
(or Cheddar cheese)
3 ounces

frisée lettuce
2 handfuls

O Preheat oven to 350°F. Chop the shallots and sauté in an oiled pan over medium heat. Once lightly browned, pour in the vinegar and let reduce.

O Slice the buns in half, if necessary. Slice the cheese. Warm the buns in the oven for 5 minutes.

O Season the patties with salt and pepper. Cook them in an oiled pan 1–2 minutes on each side. Place the cheese on the patties and melt in the oven for 2 minutes.

O Place the shallots on the bottom buns, then arrange the patties and lettuce. Top to finish.

fren'cheese

BEAUFORT AND MUSHROOM BURGER

 15 minutes prep time

 5 minutes cooking time

 Serves 2

hamburger buns
x 2 large

hamburger patties
x 2 (⅓ pound)

onion
x 1 small

mushrooms
x 8

Beaufort cheese
(or Gruyère cheese)
3 ounces

aioli
4 tablespoons

○ Preheat oven to 350°F. Quarter the mushrooms, slice the buns in half, if necessary, and slice the cheese. Chop the onion. Season the patties with salt and pepper.

○ Brown the onion in an oiled pan over medium heat, then add the mushrooms. Season with salt and pepper and sauté until golden brown. Warm the buns in the oven for 5 minutes.

○ Cook the patties in an oiled pan 1–2 minutes on each side over high heat. Place the cheese on the patties and melt in the oven for 2 minutes.

○ Spread the aioli on the buns, then arrange the patties and mushrooms. Top to finish.

SPINACH AND BLUE CHEESE BURGER

 15 minutes prep time

 25 minutes cooking time

 Serves 2

hamburger buns
x 2 large

hamburger patties
x 2 (⅓ pound)

onions
x 2 medium

crème fraîche
or Greek yogurt
1 tablespoon

Roquefort cheese
3 ounces

baby spinach
2 handfuls

○ Preheat oven to 350°F. Chop the onions and sauté in an oiled pan over medium heat. Once lightly browned, lower the heat, add salt and pepper and let caramelize for 20 minutes. Slice the buns in half, if necessary.

○ Mix the crème fraîche and cheese and heat in the microwave for 20 seconds. Warm the buns in the oven for 5 minutes.

○ Season the patties with salt and pepper, then cook in an oiled pan 1–2 minutes on each side.

○ Arrange the onions, patties, cheese sauce, and spinach on the buns. Top to finish.

fren'cheese

RACLETTE BURGER

 10 minutes prep time

 5 minutes cooking time

 Serves 2

hamburger buns
x 2 large

hamburger patties
x 2 (⅓ pound)

Raclette cheese
x 4 small slices

tartar sauce
4 tablespoons

cornichon pickles
x 4

mâche (lamb's lettuce)
2 handfuls

○ Preheat oven to 350°F. Slice the buns in half, if necessary, and cut the cornichons lengthwise. Season the patties with salt and pepper.

○ Warm the buns for 5 minutes.

○ Cook the patties in an oiled pan 1–2 minutes on each side. Place the cheese on the patties and melt in the oven for 2 minutes.

○ Spread the tartar sauce on the buns, then arrange the patties, pickles, and greens. Top to finish.

TARTIFLETTE BURGER

 15 minutes prep time

 25 minutes cooking time

 Serves 2

whole-grain rolls
x 2

hamburger patties
x 2 (⅓ pound)

Reblochon cheese
(or Camembert cheese)
x 4 small slices

onions
x 2 medium

chopped pancetta or bacon
⅓ cup

baby greens
2 handfuls

○ Preheat oven to 350°F. Chop the onions and sauté in an oiled pan over medium heat. Once lightly browned, lower the heat, add salt and pepper, and let caramelize for 20 minutes. Slice the rolls in half and warm in the oven for 3 minutes.

○ Brown the pancetta. Season the patties with salt and pepper, then cook in an oiled pan for 1 minute on each side.

○ On each bottom roll, place the onions, a patty, 2 slices of cheese, and the pancetta. Heat in the oven 2–3 minutes.

○ Add the greens, then top to finish.

MONT D'OR AND SAUSAGE BURGER

 5 minutes prep time

 5 minutes cooking time

 Serves 2

hamburger buns
x 2 large

hamburger patties
x 2 (⅓ pound)

Mont d'Or cheese
(or Brie cheese)
2 heaping tablespoons

garlic sausage
x 4 slices

O Preheat oven to 350°F. Slice the buns in half, if necessary, and warm in the oven for 3 minutes.

O Season the patties with salt and pepper, then cook in an oiled pan 1–2 minutes on each side. Top each patty with a spoonful of cheese.

O Spread the mustard on the bottom buns, add the patties, and heat in the oven 2–3 minutes. Layer the sliced sausage and greens, then top to finish.

mustard
2 tablespoons

mâche (lamb's lettuce)
2 handfuls

fren'cheese

TOMME AND RÖSTI BURGER

🔪 **10 minutes prep time**

🍲 **15 minutes cooking time**

☺ **Serves 2**

ciabatta rolls
x 2 small

hamburger patties
x 2 (⅓ pound)

Tomme cheese
(or Meunster cheese)
x 4 small slices

rösti (hash brown patties)
x 2 (packaged)

special sauce
4 tablespoons

butter lettuce
x 4 leaves

○ Preheat oven to 350°F. Slice the rolls in half. Cook the hash brown patties according to the instructions on the package.

○ Warm the rolls in the oven for 3 minutes. Season the patties with salt and pepper, then cook in an oiled pan over high heat 1–2 minutes on each side.

○ Spread the special sauce on the bottom rolls, then place the hash brown patties, hamburger patties, and cheese. Heat in the oven 2–3 minutes. Add the lettuce, then top to finish.

fren'cheese

APPLE CAMEMBERT BURGER

🔪 **10 minutes prep time**

🍲 **15 minutes cooking time**

☺ **Serves 2**

hamburger buns
x 2 large

hamburger patties
x 2 (⅓ pound)

Camembert cheese
x 4 slices

apple
x 1

aioli
4 tablespoons

mâche (lamb's lettuce)
x 2 handfuls

○ Preheat oven to 350°F. Cut the apple into thin slices, then lightly brown in a pan with a little oil.

○ Slice the buns in half, if necessary, and warm in the oven for 3 minutes.

○ Season the patties with salt and pepper, then cook in an oiled pan over high heat 1–2 minutes on each side.

○ Spread the aioli on the buns, then place the patties and cheese on the bottom buns and melt in the oven 2–3 minutes. Add the apple slices and greens, then top to finish.

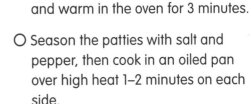

MAROILLES AND ENDIVE BURGER

 5 minutes prep time

 5 minutes cooking time

 Serves 2

hamburger buns
x 2 large

hamburger patties
x 2 (⅓ pound)

Maroilles cheese
(or Camembert cheese)
x 4 small slices

endive
x 1

mustard
2 tablespoons

cornichon pickles
x 2

O Preheat oven to 350°F. Slice the buns in half, if necessary, and cut the pickles lengthwise. Chop the endive lengthwise.

O Warm the buns in the oven for 3 minutes. Season the patties with salt and pepper, then cook in an oiled pan over high heat 1–2 minutes on each side.

O Spread the mustard on the bottom buns, then add the patties and cheese and melt in the oven 2–3 minutes.

O Add the pickles and endive, then top to finish.

MUENSTER AND SAUERKRAUT BURGER

🔪 **10 minutes prep time**

🍲 **17 minutes cooking time**

☺ **Serves 2**

hamburger buns
x 2 large

hamburger patties
x 2 (⅓ pound)

Muenster cheese
with cumin
x 4 small slices

bacon
x 6 slices

sauerkraut
1 cup

mustard
2 tablespoons

○ Rinse the sauerkraut and strain to remove all water.

○ Preheat oven to 350°F. Cook the bacon in the oven for 12 minutes. Slice the buns in half, if necessary, and warm in the oven for 5 minutes.

○ Season the patties with salt and pepper, then cook in an oiled pan 1–2 minutes on each side. Place the cheese on the patties and melt in the oven for 2 minutes.

○ Spread the mustard on the buns, then arrange the patties, bacon, and sauerkraut. Top to finish.

fren'cheese

MUSTARD BEAUFORT BURGER

 10 minutes prep time

 5 minutes cooking time

 Serves 2

hamburger buns
x 2 large

hamburger patties
x 2 (⅓ pound)

O Preheat oven to 350°F. Mix the mustard and crème fraîche, then heat for 45 seconds in the microwave.

O Thinly slice the cheese. Slice the buns in half, if necessary, then warm in the oven for 5 minutes.

Beaufort cheese
(or Gruyère cheese)
3 ounces

crème fraîche
or Greek yogurt
1 tablespoon

O Season the patties with salt and pepper, then cook in an oiled pan 1–2 minutes on each side. Place the cheese on the patties and melt in the oven for 2 minutes.

O Spread the mustard cream on the buns, then layer the patties and spinach. Top to finish.

whole-grain mustard
1 tablespoon

baby spinach
2 handfuls

PEPPERY TOMME AND CHICKEN BURGER

🔪 **10 minutes prep time**

🍲 **15 minutes cooking time**

☺ **Serves 2**

hamburger buns
x 2 large

chicken breasts
x 2 (⅓ pound)

onion
x ½ medium

red bell pepper
x ½

Tomme cheese
(or Muenster cheese)
3 ounces

arugula
2 handfuls

○ Preheat oven to 350°F. Finely chop the chicken, then add salt and pepper. Shape the chicken into patties. Cut the cheese into slices. Slice the buns in half, if necessary. Chop the onion and red bell pepper.

○ Sauté the onion in oil over medium heat. Once lightly browned, add the bell pepper and cook for 1 minute. Add salt and pepper. Warm the buns in the oven for 5 minutes.

○ Cook the patties in an oiled pan over medium heat 3–4 minutes on each side. Place the cheese on top and melt in the oven 2–3 minutes.

○ Arrange the patties, vegetable mixture, and arugula on the buns. Top to finish.

LAUGHING COW AND HAM BURGER

10 minutes prep time

5 minutes cooking time

Serves 2

hamburger buns
x 2 large

hamburger patties
x 2 (⅓ pound)

ham
x 1 slice

The Laughing Cow™
cheese
x 4 wedges

red leaf lettuce
x 4 leaves

special sauce
4 tablespoons

○ Preheat oven to 350°F. Slice the ham and the buns, if necessary, in half. Flatten out the cheese wedges.

○ Warm the buns in the oven for 5 minutes.

○ Season the patties with salt and pepper, then cook in an oiled pan 1–2 minutes on each side. Place the cheese on the patties and melt in the oven 2–3 minutes.

○ Spread the special sauce on the buns, then arrange the patties with the ham and lettuce. Top to finish.

CHICKEN TIKKA BURGER

 5 minutes prep time

 5 minutes cooking time

 Serves 2

hamburger buns
x 2 large

chicken tikka
(or grilled chicken)
x 8 pieces

tzatziki
½ cup

cucumber
x ½

cilantro
x ½ bunch

O Slice the buns in half, if necessary. Cut the cucumber into round slices.

O Heat the chicken in the oven according to the instructions on the package. Place the buns in the oven for 5 minutes before taking out the chicken.

O Spread the tzatziki on the buns, then add the cucumber, chicken, and cilantro. Top to finish.

O You can also serve this with sliced tomato and/or onion.

THAI CURRY CHICKEN BURGER

🔪 **5 minutes prep time**

🍲 **5 minutes cooking time**

☺ **Serves 2**

hamburger buns
x 2 large

chicken breasts
x 2 (⅓ pound)

Thai red curry paste
1 teaspoon

cucumber
x ¼

cilantro
x ¼ bunch

Thai sweet chili sauce
4 tablespoons

○ Preheat oven to 350°F. Cut the cucumber into thin round slices. Mince the cilantro. Finely chop the chicken and mix it with the minced cilantro and curry paste, then add salt and pepper. Shape into patties.

○ Slice the buns in half, if necessary, and warm in the oven for 5 minutes. Cook the patties in an oiled pan over medium heat 3–4 minutes on each side.

○ Spread the chili sauce on the buns, then arrange the patties and cucumber. Top to finish.

BANH MI BURGER

 🔪 **10 minutes prep time**

 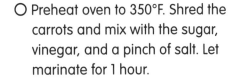 **8 minutes cooking time**
1 hour marinating time

 😊 **Serves 2**

hamburger buns
x 2 large

sausage meat
⅔ pound

carrots
x 2 medium

brown sugar
1 tablespoon

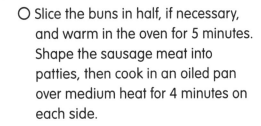

○ Preheat oven to 350°F. Shred the
carrots and mix with the sugar,
vinegar, and a pinch of salt. Let
marinate for 1 hour.

○ Slice the buns in half, if necessary,
and warm in the oven for 5 minutes.
Shape the sausage meat into
patties, then cook in an oiled pan
over medium heat for 4 minutes on
each side.

○ Arrange the patties on the buns,
then add the marinated carrots and
cilantro. Top to finish.

○ You can also serve this with
mayonnaise.

white vinegar
2 tablespoons

cilantro
x ¼ bunch

HAWAIIAN BURGER

 10 minutes prep time

 20 minutes cooking time

 Serves 2

hamburger buns
x 2 large

sausage meat
⅔ pound

pineapple
x 4 slices

bacon
x 6 slices

Thai sweet chili sauce
4 tablespoons

red leaf lettuce
x 4 leaves

○ Shape the sausage meat into patties.

○ Preheat oven to 350°F. Cook the bacon in the oven for 12 minutes. Caramelize the pineapple in an oiled pan. Slice the buns in half, if necessary, and warm in the oven for 5 minutes.

○ Cook the patties in an oiled pan over medium heat for 4 minutes on each side.

○ Spread the chili sauce on the buns, then arrange the patties, pineapple, bacon, and lettuce. Top to finish.

TERIYAKI BEEF BURGER

 10 minutes prep time

 5 minutes cooking time

 Serves 2

hamburger buns
x 2 large

hamburger patties
x 2 (⅓ pound)

teriyaki sauce
3 tablespoons

mayonnaise
2 tablespoons

white cabbage
1 cup

jalapeño
x 1

○ Preheat oven to 350°F. Chop the cabbage and jalapeño, then mix with the mayonnaise, salt, and pepper.

○ Season the patties with salt and pepper. Slice the buns in half, if necessary, and warm in the oven for 5 minutes.

○ Heat oil in a pan, then cook the patties over high heat for 2 minutes. Flip and cook for 1½ minutes more. Add the teriyaki sauce and cook for 30 seconds.

○ Layer the patties and spicy mayo cabbage on the buns. Top to finish.

YAKITORI CHICKEN BURGER

 15 minutes prep time

 5 minutes cooking time

 Serves 2

hamburger buns
x 2 large

chicken breasts
x 2 (⅓ pound)

scallions
x 3

ginger
2 tablespoons

teriyaki sauce
3 tablespoons

coleslaw
1 cup

O Preheat oven to 350°F. Finely chop the chicken and scallions, then shred the ginger and mix to combine. Season the chicken mixture with salt and pepper, then shape into patties.

O Slice the buns in half, if necessary, and warm in the oven for 5 minutes. Cook the patties in an oiled pan over medium heat 3–4 minutes on each side. Add the teriyaki sauce 1 minute before removing from the heat.

O Arrange the patties on the buns and add the coleslaw. Top to finish.

TONKATSU BURGER

 15 minutes prep time

 8 minutes cooking time

 Serves 2

hamburger buns
x 2 large

boneless pork chops
x 2 (⅓ pound)

egg
x 1

flour
¼ cup

panko
(Japanese breadcrumbs)
½ cup

tonkatsu sauce
(or barbecue sauce)
4 tablespoons

O Preheat oven to 350°F. Between two sheets of parchment paper, flatten the pork with a rolling pin. Season with salt and pepper. Beat the egg, adding salt and pepper.

O Dip the pork into the flour, then into the egg, then into the panko.

O In an oiled pan, cook the pork over medium heat 3–4 minutes on each side. Slice the buns in half, if necessary, and warm in the oven for 5 minutes.

O Spread the tonkatsu sauce on the buns, then place the breaded pork. Top to finish.

TEX-MEX BURGER

  15 minutes prep time

 18 minutes cooking time

Serves 2

hamburger buns
x 2 large

chicken breasts
x 2 (⅓ pound)

○ Preheat oven to 350°F. Finely chop the chicken, then add salt, pepper, and 1 teaspoon of the fajita seasoning. Shape into patties.

○ Chop the onion and red bell pepper. Sauté the onion in oil over medium heat. Once lightly browned, add in the bell pepper, salt, pepper, and the rest of the fajita seasoning. Cook for 1 minute.

onion
x ½ medium

red bell pepper
x ½

○ Slice the buns in half, if necessary, and warm in the oven for 5 minutes. Cook the patties in an oiled pan over medium heat 3–4 minutes on each side.

○ Spread the guacamole on the buns, then layer the patties and vegetable mixture. Top to finish.

fajita seasoning
2 teaspoons

guacamole
¾ cup

PINEAPPLE MANGO CHICKEN BURGER

 15 minutes prep time

 14 minutes cooking time

 Serves 2

hamburger buns
x 2 large

chicken breasts
x 2 (⅓ pound)

pineapple
x 2 slices

mango chutney
2 tablespoons

cilantro
x ½ bunch

avocado
x 1 ripe

○ Preheat oven to 350°F. Mince the cilantro. Finely chop the chicken, then add salt, pepper, and the minced cilantro. Shape into patties.

○ Caramelize the pineapple in an oiled pan. Set aside. In the oiled pan, cook the patties over medium heat 3–4 minutes on each side. Slice the buns in half, if necessary, and warm in the oven for 5 minutes.

○ Spread the chutney on the buns, then layer a patty, a pineapple slice, and a sliced avocado half on each bottom bun. Top to finish.

KOFTA BURGER

 15 minutes prep time

 6 minutes cooking time

 Serves 2

poppy seed rolls
x 2

hamburger patties
x 2 (⅓ pound)

ground cumin
2 teaspoons

onion
½ small

cilantro
x ½ bunch

Greek-style
eggplant salad
½ cup

○ Preheat oven to 350°F. Chop the onion, mince half of the cilantro, and combine with the hamburger patties, cumin, salt, and pepper. Reshape into patties.

○ Heat oil in a pan and cook the patties 2–3 minutes on each side over high heat.

○ Slice the buns in half, if necessary, and warm in the oven for 5 minutes.

○ Spread the eggplant salad on the buns, then arrange the patties and the remaining cilantro. Top to finish.

PESTO CAPRESE BURGER

  10 minutes prep time

 10 minutes cooking time

 **Serves 2**

ciabatta rolls
x 2 small

hamburger patties
x 2 (⅓ pound)

○ Preheat oven to 350°F. Cut the sun-dried tomatoes into strips and slice the cheese. Season the patties with salt and pepper. Slice the rolls in half and warm in the oven for 3 minutes.

○ Heat oil in a pan and cook the patties 1–2 minutes over high heat on each side. Add the cheese slices to the patties and melt in the oven 2–3 minutes.

mozzarella cheese
5 ounces

sun-dried tomatoes
x 6

○ Spread the pesto on the rolls, then arrange the patties, tomatoes, and arugula. Top to finish.

pesto
2 tablespoons

arugula
2 handfuls

SUN-DRIED TOMATO CHICKEN BURGER

15 minutes prep time

10 minutes cooking time

Serves 2

hamburger buns
x 2 large

chicken breasts
x 2 (⅓ pound)

○ Preheat oven to 350°F. Cut the sun-dried tomatoes into strips. Finely chop the chicken and season with salt and pepper, then shape into patties.

○ Slice the buns in half, if necessary, and warm in the oven for 3 minutes.

○ Heat oil in a pan and cook the patties over medium heat 3–4 minutes on each side.

○ Spread the baba ghanoush on the buns, then add a patty and a goat cheese round to each bottom bun. Heat in the oven 2–3 minutes. Add the sun-dried tomatoes and greens, then top to finish.

goat cheese rounds
x 2

sun-dried tomatoes
x 6

baba ghanoush
½ cup

baby greens
2 handfuls

MINT FETA CHICKEN BURGER

 15 minutes prep time

 10 minutes cooking time

 Serves 2

hamburger buns
x 2 large

chicken breasts
x 2 (⅓ pound)

○ Preheat oven to 350°F. Thinly slice the cheese and the tomato. Finely chop the chicken, season with salt and pepper, then shape into patties.

feta cheese
3 ounces

tomato
x 1 medium

○ Slice the buns in half, if necessary, and warm in the oven for 5 minutes.

○ Heat oil in a pan and cook the patties over medium heat 3–4 minutes on each side.

○ Spread tzatziki on the buns, then arrange the patties, tomato slices, feta, and mint leaves. Top to finish.

mint
x 4 sprigs

tzatziki
½ cup

ENGLISH FRY-UP BURGER

🔪 **20 minutes prep time**

🍲 **20 minutes cooking time**

☺ **Serves 2**

English muffins
x 2

sausage meat
½ pound

○ Preheat oven to 350°F. Shape the sausage meat into patties. Cook the bacon in the oven for 12 minutes.

cheddar cheese
x 2 slices

eggs
x 2

○ Heat oil in a pan and cook the patties over medium heat 2–3 minutes on each side. In another pan, fry the eggs. Heat the beans in the microwave.

○ Slice the English muffins in half and warm in the oven for 3 minutes. Place the cheese on the bottom halves, then warm 1–2 minutes more, until the cheese melts.

bacon
x 6 slices

baked beans
x ½ can

○ Place a patty on each cheesy muffin bottom, then layer with 3 bacon slices and an egg. Top to finish and serve with the beans.

SURF AND TURF BURGER

 15 minutes prep time

 8 minutes cooking time

 Serves 2

hamburger buns
x 2 large

sausage meat
⅔ pound

shrimp
x 8 (frozen)

garlic
x 1 clove

mayonnaise
2 tablespoons

alfalfa sprouts
x ½ container

○ Preheat oven to 350°F. Crush the garlic clove. Thaw the shrimp, then peel and devein. Mix them with salt, pepper, and the crushed garlic. Refrigerate for 15 minutes.

○ Shape the sausage meat into patties. Heat oil in a pan and cook the patties over medium heat 3–4 minutes on each side.

○ Slice the buns in half, if necessary, and warm in the oven for 5 minutes. Sauté the shrimp in oil for 2 minutes.

○ Spread the mayonnaise on the buns, then layer the patties, shrimp, and sprouts. Top to finish.

SALMON BAGEL

 10 minutes prep time

 10 minutes cooking time

 Serves 2

bagels
x 2

salmon fillets
x 2 (½ pound)

cream cheese
⅓ cup

red onion
x ¼ medium

capers
2 tablespoons

arugula
2 handfuls

○ Preheat oven to 350°F.

○ In a pot, cover the salmon with cold water and generously season with salt and pepper. Bring to a boil, then turn off the heat and let cool in the water. Dry the salmon using paper towels, then remove the skin and any bones.

○ Chop the onion. Slice the bagels in half and warm in the oven 5–7 minutes.

○ Spread the cream cheese on the bagels, then arrange the salmon, onion, capers, and arugula. Top to finish.

TZATZIKI DILL SALMON BURGER

 10 minutes prep time

 10 minutes cooking time

 Serves 2

whole-grain rolls
x 2

salmon fillets
x 2 (⅓ pound)

iceberg lettuce
2 handfuls

tzatziki
½ cup

dill
x 4 sprigs

lemon
x ½

○ In a pot, cover the salmon with cold water and add salt, pepper, and the juice from the lemon. Bring to a boil, then turn off the heat and let cool in the water. Dry the salmon using paper towels, then remove the skin and any bones.

○ Preheat oven to 350°F. Slice the rolls in half and warm in the oven for 5 minutes.

○ Spread the tzatziki on the rolls, then layer the salmon, dill, and lettuce. Top to finish.

AVOCADO SALMON BURGER

 10 minutes prep time

 3 minutes cooking time

 Serves 2

hamburger buns
x 2 large

salmon fillets
x 2 (⅓ pound)

cucumber
x ¼

avocado
x 1 ripe

sweet soy sauce
3 tablespoons

mayonnaise
4 tablespoons

○ Preheat oven to 350°F. Marinate the salmon in the soy sauce for 10 minutes. Thinly slice the cucumber and the avocado. Slice the buns in half, if necessary, and warm in the oven for 5 minutes.

○ Preheat a pan without oil, then cook the salmon over medium heat for 1½ minutes on each side. Let cool in the pan.

○ Spread the mayonnaise on the buns, then arrange the avocado, salmon, and cucumber. Top to finish.

○ Try spicing it up by adding wasabi to the mayo.

FISH AND CHIPS BURGER

 20 minutes prep time

5 minutes cooking time

Serves 2

sesame rolls
x 2

cod fillets
x 2 (⅓ pound)

○ Preheat oven to 350°F. Heat 1 cup of oil in a pan.

○ Season the cod fillets with salt and pepper. Mix the flour, egg white, beer, salt, and pepper. Coat the fillets in the batter and fry for 5 minutes.

○ Slice the buns in half, if necessary, and warm in the oven for 5 minutes. Serve the fillets on the buns, topped with a handful of potato chips.

○ You can also spread aioli on the buns.

flour with two teaspoons
baking powder
¾ cup

egg white
x 1

beer
½ cup

salt and vinegar potato chips
3 ounces

TARTAR FRIED FISH BURGER

 10 minutes prep time

 15 minutes cooking time

 Serves 2

hamburger buns
x 2 large

breaded fish fillets
x 4 (packaged)

○ Chop the capers and pickles, then add to the tartar sauce. Slice the buns in half, if necessary. Heat up the breaded fish in the oven according to the instructions on the package. Place the buns in the oven for 5 minutes before taking out the fish.

tartar sauce
5 tablespoons

capers
½ tablespoon

○ Spread the tartar sauce on the buns, then add 2 fish fillets and 2 lettuce leaves to each bottom bun. Top to finish.

○ You can substitute mayonnaise for the tartar sauce.

pickles
x 3

butter lettuce
x 4 leaves

BACALAO AND PIQUILLO BURGER

 10 minutes prep time

 6 minutes cooking time

 Serves 2

poppy seed rolls
x 2

desalted bacalao
(salt cod)
x 2 fillets (⅓ pound)

flour
¼ cup

aioli
4 tablespoons

piquillo peppers
x 6

fresh basil
x 4 sprigs

O Preheat oven to 350°F. Cut open the piquillo peppers and remove any seeds. Dab to remove excess liquid. Slice the buns in half, if necessary.

O Season the cod with pepper, then cover with the flour. Tap to remove any excess flour. Pan-fry in an oiled pan 2–3 minutes on each side over medium heat. Drain on paper towels to soak up any extra oil. Heat the buns in the oven for 5 minutes.

O Spread the aioli on the buns, then arrange the fish, piquillo peppers, and basil. Top to finish.

MAYO TUNA BURGER

 15 minutes prep time

 3 minutes cooking time

☺ **Serves 2**

whole-grain rolls
x 2

tuna
6 ounces

scallions
x 2 (with stalks)

mayonnaise
4 tablespoons

tomatoes
x 2 medium

egg
x 1

○ Preheat oven to 350°F. Chop the scallions, including the stalks. Drain the tuna to remove all excess water. Mix with the scallions, egg, salt, and pepper. Slice the tomato. Slice the rolls in half and warm in the oven for 5 minutes.

○ Shape the tuna mixture into patties, then cook in an oiled pan 1–2 minutes on each side over medium heat.

○ Spread the mayonnaise on the rolls, then arrange the tomato and patties. Top to finish.

SHRIMP MEZE BURGER

 20 minutes prep time

 5 minutes cooking time

 Serves 2

hamburger buns
x 2 small

shrimp
½ pound (frozen)

scallions
x 2

taramosalata
4 tablespoons

cucumber
x ¼

alfalfa sprouts
x ½ container

○ Preheat oven to 350°F. Cut the cucumber into thin round slices.

○ Thaw the shrimp, then peel, devein, and chop. Coarsely chop the scallions, then mix with the shrimp. Season with salt and pepper. Using wet hands, shape into patties.

○ Slice the buns in half, if necessary, and warm in the oven for 5 minutes. Cook the patties in an oiled pan 1–2 minutes on each side over medium heat.

○ Spread the taramosalata on the buns, then arrange the patties, cucumber, and sprouts. Top to finish.

FRIED CALAMARI BURGER WITH AIOLI

 5 minutes prep time

  15 minutes cooking time

Serves 2

hamburger buns
x 2 large

fried calamari
x 12 (frozen)

O Chop the capers, mince the parsley, and then mix them with the aioli. Slice the buns in half, if necessary.

O Heat up the calamari in the oven according to the instructions on the package. Place the buns in the oven for 5 minutes before taking out the calamari.

O Spread the aioli mixture on the buns and add the lettuce. Then arrange the calamari, overlapping 2 rows of 3 rings each. Top to finish.

aioli
5 tablespoons

fresh parsley
x 2 sprigs

capers
1 tablespoon

butter lettuce
x 2 leaves

CHORIZO COD BURGER

10 minutes prep time

15 minutes cooking time

Serves 2

seeded rolls
x 2

cod loins
x 2 (⅓ pound)

green bell pepper
x 1

onion
x 1 medium

chorizo
x 12 slices

special sauce
4 tablespoons

O Preheat oven to 350°F. Chop the onion and bell pepper. Heat oil in a pan and sear the chorizo over medium heat. Remove the chorizo from the pan and set aside. In the same pan, sauté the onion. Once lightly browned, add the bell pepper and cook for 1 minute. Slice the buns in half, if necessary, and warm in the oven for 5 minutes.

O Season the cod with salt and pepper. Heat oil in a pan and cook the cod 1–2 minutes on each side over medium heat.

O Spread the special sauce on the buns, then arrange the vegetable mixture, cod, and chorizo. Top to finish.

veggie

PESTO GRILLED VEGGIES

 10 minutes prep time

 15 minutes cooking time

 Serves 2

hamburger buns
x 2 large

grilled vegetables
⅔ pound (frozen)

onion
x ½ medium

goat cheese rounds
x 2

pesto
2 tablespoons

○ Preheat oven to 350°F. Thaw the vegetables. Chop the onion.

○ Sauté the onion in oil over medium heat. Once it is lightly browned, add the vegetables and heat them up. Off the heat, mix in the pesto, salt, and pepper.

○ Slice the buns in half, if necessary, and warm in the oven for 3 minutes.

○ Place the vegetables on the bottom buns and top each with a goat cheese round. Add the top buns, then heat in the oven for 2 minutes.

veggie

EGGPLANT PARM BURGER

🔪 **15 minutes prep time**

🍲 **50 minutes cooking time**

☺ **Serves 2**

poppy seed rolls
x 2

eggplant
x 1 large

onion
x 1 medium

mozzarella cheese
4 ounces

tomato puree
⅔ cup

fresh basil
several sprigs

○ Preheat oven to 425°F. Cut the eggplant into round slices and add salt. Let sit for 15 minutes to remove water. Brush the eggplant with oil and bake 30–35 minutes, turning over occasionally.

○ Chop the onion and brown in an oiled pan over medium heat. Add the tomato puree, salt, and pepper, and simmer for 15 minutes.

○ Lower the oven to 350°F. Slice the buns in half, if necessary, and warm in the oven for 3 minutes.

○ Coat the buns with the tomato blend, then add the eggplant slices and cheese to the bottom buns. Melt in the oven 2–3 minutes. Add the basil leaves and top to finish.

veggie

MUSHROOM SPINACH BURGER

 15 minutes prep time

 15 minutes cooking time

 Serves 2

hamburger buns
x 2 large

mushrooms
x 4 large

herb butter
3 tablespoons

mozzarella cheese
4 ounces

baby spinach
5 cups

○ Preheat oven to 350°F. Cut the cheese into two slices.

○ Sauté the mushrooms in an oiled pan for 5 minutes over medium heat. Once browned, add half the herb butter, salt, and pepper. Stir and set aside.

○ In the same pan, cook the spinach 1–2 minutes in a little oil, then add the remaining herb butter. Season with salt and pepper, and stir. Slice the buns in half, if necessary, and warm in the oven for 3 minutes.

○ Place the mushrooms and cheese on the bottom buns, then heat in the oven 2–3 minutes. Add the spinach, then top to finish.

veggie

HUMMUS BEET BURGER

🔪 **10 minutes prep time**

🍲 **5 minutes cooking time**

☺ **Serves 2**

hamburger buns
x 2 large

cooked beet
x 1 large

○ Preheat oven to 350°F. Slice the buns in half, if necessary. Cut the tomato into slices and the beet into thick slices. Grate the cheese.

○ Warm the buns in the oven for 5 minutes.

○ Spread the hummus on the buns, then arrange the beet slices, tomato, cheese, and greens. Top to finish.

Comté cheese
(or Gruyère cheese)
3 ounces

tomato
x 1 medium

hummus
½ cup

baby greens
2 handfuls

VEGGIE PESTO CAPRESE BURGER

5 minutes prep time

5 minutes cooking time

Serves 2

hamburger buns
x 2 large

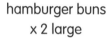

mozzarella cheese
5 ounces

tomato
x 1 medium

pesto
2 tablespoons

arugula
2 handfuls

○ Preheat oven to 350°F. Slice the buns in half, if necessary. Cut the tomato into slices and the cheese into 2 thick slices.

○ Warm the buns in the oven for 5 minutes.

○ Spread the pesto on the buns, then add the cheese slices and heat in the oven 1–2 minutes. Add the tomato and arugula, then top to finish.

○ You can also season the arugula with balsamic vinaigrette.

veggie

TZATZIKI CHICKPEA BURGER

 15 minutes prep time

 15 minutes cooking time

 Serves 2

hamburger buns
x 2 large

chickpeas (cooked)
12 ounces

○ Preheat oven to 375°F. Strain the chickpeas, then blend in a food processor along with the cumin seeds, salt, and pepper. Shape into patties. Bake for 10 minutes.

cumin seeds
2 teaspoons

tomato
x 1 medium

○ Dice the tomato and chop the scallions, then mix to combine with salt and pepper.

○ Slice the buns in half, if necessary, and warm in the oven for 5 minutes.

○ Spread the tzatziki on the buns, then arrange the patties and tomato salad. Top to finish.

scallions
x 1½

tzatziki
½ cup

veggie

GOUDA NAVY BEAN BURGER

 15 minutes prep time

 10 minutes cooking time

 Serves 2

hamburger buns
x 2 large

navy beans
(cooked or canned)
12 ounces

breadcrumbs
2 tablespoons

special sauce
4 tablespoons

tomato
x 1 medium

Gouda cheese
3 ounces

○ Blend the strained navy beans in a food processor. Add salt, pepper, and the breadcrumbs. Shape into patties.

○ Preheat oven to 350°F. Slice the buns in half, if necessary. Cut the tomato into slices and thinly slice the cheese.

○ Heat oil in a pan and cook the patties 1–2 minutes on each side. Warm the buns in the oven for 5 minutes. Place the cheese on the patties and melt in the oven for 3 minutes.

○ Spread the special sauce on the buns, then layer the patties and tomato slices. Top to finish.

SWEET POTATO BURGER

 15 minutes prep time

 1 hour cooking time

 Serves 2

hamburger buns
x 2 large

sweet potato
⅔ pound

kidney beans
(cooked or canned)
5 ounces

baba ghanoush
4 tablespoons

breadcrumbs
2 tablespoons

red leaf lettuce
x 4 leaves

○ Preheat oven to 400°F. Wrap the sweet potato in aluminum foil and bake for 50 minutes. Mash the potato flesh with a fork, then mix with the strained kidney beans and breadcrumbs. Add salt and pepper. Shape into patties. Heat oil in a pan and brown the patties 2–3 minutes on each side over high heat.

○ Lower the oven temperature to 350°F. Slice the buns in half, if necessary, and warm in the oven for 5 minutes.

○ Spread the baba ghanoush on the buns, then arrange the patties and lettuce. Top to finish.

veggie

PICCALILLI VEGGIE BURGER

 5 minutes prep time

 15 minutes cooking time

 Serves 2

hamburger buns
x 2 large

veggie burgers
x 2 (packaged)

piccalilli sauce
2 tablespoons

cheddar cheese
x 2 slices

tomato
x 1 medium

butter lettuce
x 2 leaves

○ Preheat oven to 350°F. Slice the buns in half, if necessary. Cut the tomato into slices.

○ Heat up the veggie burgers according to the instructions on the package. Warm the buns in the oven for 3 minutes. Then place the cheese on the bottom buns and heat for 2 more minutes.

○ Spread the piccalilli sauce on the buns, then arrange the veggie burgers, tomato, and lettuce. Top to finish.

GUACAMOLE LENTIL BURGER

 15 minutes prep time

 22 minutes cooking time

 Serves 2

Whole-grain rolls
x 2 small

red lentils
3 ounces

carrot
x 1 medium

breadcrumbs
2 tablespoons

guacamole
4 tablespoons

cilantro
x ¼ bunch

O Cook the lentils for 12 minutes in boiling water, then strain. Shred the carrot. Mix with the lentils, then add the breadcrumbs, salt, and pepper. Shape into patties.

O Preheat oven to 350°F. Slice the rolls in half and warm in the oven for 5 minutes.

O Heat oil in a pan and brown the patties 3–4 minutes on each side over high heat.

O Spread the rolls with the guacamole, then arrange the patties and cilantro. Top to finish.

ZUCCHINI FRITTATA BURGER

 15 minutes prep time

 10 minutes cooking time

 Serves 2

ciabatta rolls
x 2 small

zucchini
x 1 large

eggs
x 3

feta cheese
3 ounces

mint
x ½ bunch

aioli
4 tablespoons

O Shred the zucchini and chop the mint. Cook the zucchini for 1 minute in the microwave. Strain well. Beat the eggs, then mix in the zucchini, mint, and crumbled feta. Add salt and pepper.

O Heat oil in a pan and cook the mixture over medium heat about 3 minutes. Cut the frittata into four pieces, then flip and cook 2–3 minutes more.

O Preheat oven to 350°F. Slice the rolls in half and warm in the oven for 5 minutes.

O Spread the aioli on the rolls, then add the frittata. Top to finish.

veggie

FALAFEL BURGER

seeded rolls
x 2

falafel
x 8 small

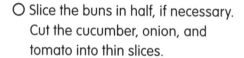

🔪 **5 minutes prep time**

🍲 **10 minutes cooking time**

☺ **Serves 2**

hummus
½ cup

tomato
x 1 medium

○ Slice the buns in half, if necessary. Cut the cucumber, onion, and tomato into thin slices.

○ Heat up the falafel in the oven according to the instructions on the package. Place the buns in the oven for 5 minutes before taking out the falafel.

○ Spread the hummus on the buns, then arrange the onion, tomato, cucumber, and falafel. Top to finish.

cucumber
x ¼

red onion
x ½ medium

veggie
SPANISH TORTILLA BURGER

🔪 **15 minutes prep time**

🍲 **40 minutes cooking time**

☺ **Serves 2**

hamburger buns
x 2 large

eggs
x 4

potatoes
x 2 medium

onion
x 1 small

mayonnaise
4 tablespoons

butter lettuce
x 4 leaves

○ Boil the potatoes in water for 30 minutes, then cut into thin round slices. Beat the eggs, adding salt and pepper.

○ Chop and then sauté the onion in an oiled pan over medium heat, then add the potatoes, salt, and pepper. Let brown. Add a little oil, then pour in the beaten eggs. Cook over low heat 5–8 minutes. Place a plate over the pan to flip, then cook 3–4 minutes on the other side. Cut the tortilla into circular "burgers."

○ Preheat the oven to 350°F. Slice the buns in half, if necessary, and heat in the oven for 5 minutes.

○ Coat the buns with the mayonnaise, then arrange the tortilla burgers and lettuce. Top to finish.

SOY TOFU BURGER

 10 minutes prep time

 10 minutes cooking time

 Serves 2

hamburger buns
x 2 large

tofu
6 ounces

carrots
x 2 small

zucchini
x 1 medium

garlic
x 2 cloves

sweet soy sauce
3 tablespoons

○ Preheat oven to 350°F. Julienne the carrots and zucchini and crush the garlic. Slice the tofu in half and season with salt and pepper.

○ Heat oil in a pan and brown the tofu 2–3 minutes on each side over medium heat. Set aside. In the same pan, add a little more oil, then cook the vegetables, garlic, and soy sauce over high heat 2–3 minutes. The vegetables should remain crisp.

○ Slice the buns in half, if necessary, and heat in the oven for 5 minutes.

○ Place the tofu slices and vegetables on the buns, then top to finish.

FOIE GRAS BURGER

15 minutes prep time

30 minutes cooking time

Serves 2

hamburger buns
x 2 large

hamburger patties
x 2 (⅓ pound)

O Chop the onions and sauté in an oiled pan over medium heat. Once lightly browned, lower the heat, add salt and pepper, and let caramelize for 20 minutes. Add the balsamic vinegar and let reduce. Set aside.

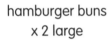

foie gras
x 4 slices (2 ounces)

onions
x 2 medium

O Preheat oven to 350°F. In another pan, quickly sear the foie gras on both sides to a golden brown. Season the foie gras and patties with salt and pepper. Then cook the patties in an oiled pan over high heat for 2 minutes on each side. Slice the buns in half, if necessary, and warm in the oven for 5 minutes.

O Arrange the onions on the bottom buns, then layer the patties, foie gras, and arugula. Top to finish.

balsamic vinegar
2 tablespoons

arugula
2 handfuls

PARMESAN DUCK BURGER

 20 minutes prep time

 10 minutes cooking time

 Serves 2

hamburger buns
x 2 large

duck breast
⅔ pound

herb butter
4 tablespoons

Parmesan cheese
2 ounces

mâche (lamb's lettuce)
2 handfuls

O Remove the skin from the duck breast and finely chop the meat. Mix with salt, pepper, and 2 tablespoons of grated Parmesan. Shape into patties. Shave the rest of the cheese.

O Preheat oven to 350°F. Heat oil in a pan and cook the patties 2–3 minutes on each side over medium heat.

O Slice the buns in half, if necessary, and warm in the oven for 5 minutes. Heat the herb butter in the microwave for 20 seconds.

O Coat the buns with the herb butter, then arrange the patties, Parmesan shavings, and greens. Top to finish.

FOIE GRAS AND DUCK BURGER

 20 minutes prep time

 10 minutes cooking time

 Serves 2

poppy seed rolls
x 2

duck breast
⅔ pound

foie gras
x 2 slices (2 ounces)

mushrooms
x 8

baby spinach
4 cups

crème fraîche
or Greek yogurt
1 tablespoon

○ Remove the skin from the duck breast and finely chop the meat. Season with salt and pepper, then shape into patties. Chop the mushrooms.

○ Heat oil in a pan and sauté the chopped mushrooms over medium heat. Add the crème fraîche and let reduce. Add the spinach, stirring. Remove from the heat. Season with salt and pepper.

○ Preheat oven to 350°F. Heat oil in a pan and cook the patties 2–3 minutes on each side over medium heat. Slice the buns in half, if necessary, and warm in the oven for 5 minutes.

○ Place the vegetable mixture on the bottom buns, then add the patties and foie gras. Top to finish.

HONEY MUSTARD DUCK CONFIT BURGER

 20 minutes prep time

 10 minutes cooking time

 Serves 2

ciabatta rolls
x 2 small

duck confit
x 2 legs

○ Chop the onion. Mix the mustard and honey.

○ Heat the duck legs in a pan over low heat, turning occasionally. When the skin is golden brown, remove the duck and add the onion to the pan. Cook until caramelized, about 15 minutes. Shred the duck meat, then blend with the onion and season with salt and pepper.

onion
x 1 medium

whole-grain mustard
2 tablespoons

○ Preheat oven to 350°F. Slice the rolls in half and warm in the oven for 5 minutes.

○ Spread the honey mustard on the rolls, then arrange the shredded duck confit and lettuce. Top to finish.

honey
½ tablespoon

frisée lettuce
2 handfuls

ingredient index

AIOLI
Apple Camembert Burger 45
Bacalao and Piquillo Burger.....................97
Beaufort and Mushroom Burger............ 33
Chicken Caesar Burger 27
Fried Calamari Burger with Aioli............103
Zucchini Frittata Burger 127

ALFALFA SPROUTS
Shrimp Meze Burger..............................101
Surf and Turf Burger 85

ANCHOVIES
Chicken Caesar Burger 27

APPLES
Apple Camembert Burger 45

ARUGULA
Foie Gras Burger..................................135
Peppery Tomme and Chicken
     Burger.. 53
Pesto Caprese Burger............................77
Salmon Bagel......................................87
Veggie Pesto Caprese Burger 115

AVOCADO
Avocado Salmon Burger 91
Guacamole Lentil Burger 125
Pineapple Mango Chicken Burger 73
Tex-Mex Burger 71

BABA GHANOUSH
Sun-Dried Tomato Chicken
     Burger...79
Sweet Potato Burger..............................121

BABY GREENS
Hummus Beet Burger..............................113
Sun-Dried Tomato Chicken
     Burger...79
Tartiflette Burger 39

BACON
Bacon Cheeseburger...............................11
Chicken BLT... 25
English Fry-Up Burger 83
Hawaiian Burger 63
Muenster and Sauerkraut
     Burger...49
Tartiflette Burger 39

BARBECUE SAUCE
Bacon Cheeseburger................................11
Chicken Nugget Burger............................23
Onion Ring Burger 21
Pulled Pork and Red Cabbage 19
Tonkatsu Burger.....................................69

BASIL
Bacalao and Piquillo Burger.....................97
Eggplant Parm Burger.............................109
Pizza Burger...15

BEANS
English Fry-Up Burger 83
Gouda Navy Bean Burger........................119
Sweet Potato Burger..............................121

BEAUFORT CHEESE
Beaufort and Mushroom Burger............ 33
Mustard Beaufort Burger 51

BEEF, GROUND
Apple Camembert Burger 45
Bacon Cheeseburger 11
Beaufort and Mushroom Burger............ 33
Burger with Fried Onions and Pickles........5
Cantal and Shallot Burger........................ 31
Cheeseburger...7
Cheese-Stuffed Burger 13
Double Cheeseburger 9
Foie Gras Burger..................................135
Hot Dog Burger.....................................29
Kofta Burger...75
Laughing Cow and Ham Burger 55
Maroilles and Endive Burger 47
Mont d'Or and Sausage Burger 41
Muenster and Sauerkraut Burger 49
Mustard Beaufort Burger 51
Onion Ring Burger 21
Pesto Caprese Burger............................77
Pizza Burger...15
Raclette Burger......................................37
Spinach and Blue Cheese Burger 35
Tartiflette Burger 39
Teriyaki Beef Burger 65
Tomme and Rösti Burger 43

BEEF, STEAK
Spicy Cheesesteak 17

BEER
Fish and Chips Burger 93

BEETS
Hummus Beet Burger..............................113

BELL PEPPERS
Bacalao and Piquillo Burger.....................97
Chorizo Cod Burger 105
Peppery Tomme and Chicken
     Burger.. 53
Tex-Mex Burger 71

BREADCRUMBS
Gouda Navy Bean Burger........................119
Guacamole Lentil Burger 125
Sweet Potato Burger..............................121
Tonkatsu Burger.....................................69

CABBAGE
Teriyaki Beef Burger 65
Muenster and Sauerkraut Burger 49
Pulled Pork and Red Cabbage 19
Yakitori Chicken Burger 67

CALAMARI
Fried Calamari Burger with Aioli.............103

CAMEMBERT CHEESE
Apple Camembert Burger 45

CANTAL CHEESE
Cantal and Shallot Burger........................ 31

CAPERS
Fried Calamari Burger with Aioli............103
Salmon Bagel......................................87
Tartar Fried Fish Burger 95

CARROTS
Banh Mi Burger.....................................61
Guacamole Lentil Burger 125
Pulled Pork and Red Cabbage 19
Soy Tofu Burger....................................133

CHEDDAR CHEESE
Bacon Cheeseburger 11
Cheeseburger...7
Cheese-Stuffed Burger 13
Double Cheeseburger 9
English Fry-Up Burger 83
Spicy Cheesesteak 17
Sweet Potato Burger..............................121

CHICKEN
Chicken BLT... 25
Chicken Caesar Burger 27
Chicken Nugget Burger............................23
Chicken Tikka Burger 57
Mint Feta Chicken Burger 81
Mustard Beaufort Burger 51
Peppery Tomme and Chicken Burger....... 53
Pineapple Mango Chicken
     Burger...73
Sun-Dried Tomato Chicken
     Burger...79
Tex-Mex Burger 71
Thai Curry Chicken Burger 59
Yakitori Chicken Burger 67

CHICKPEAS
Tzatziki Chickpea Burger.........................117

CHILI SAUCE
Hawaiian Burger 63
Thai Curry Chicken Burger 59

CHORIZO
Chorizo Cod Burger 105
Pizza Burger...15

CILANTRO
Banh Mi Burger.................................... 61
Chicken Tikka Burger 57
Guacamole Lentil Burger 125
Kofta Burger...75
Pineapple Mango Chicken
     Burger...73
Thai Curry Chicken Burger 59

COD
Bacalao and Piquillo Burger.....................97
Chorizo Cod Burger 105
Fish and Chips Burger 93

COLESLAW
Yakitori Chicken Burger 67

COMTÉ CHEESE
Hummus Beet Burger..............................113

CREAM CHEESE
Salmon Bagel......................................87

CRÈME FRAÎCHE
Foie Gras and Duck Burger.....................139
Mustard Beaufort Burger 51
Spinach and Blue Cheese Burger 35

CUCUMBER
Avocado Salmon Burger 91
Chicken Tikka Burger 57
Falafel Burger......................................129
Thai Curry Chicken Burger 59
Shrimp Meze Burger..............................101

CUMIN
Muenster and Sauerkraut Burger 49
Gouda Navy Bean Burger........................119

Kofta Burger 75
Tzatziki Chickpea Burger 117

CURRY PASTE
Thai Curry Chicken Burger 59

DILL
Tzatziki Dill Salmon Burger 89

DUCK
Foie Gras and Duck Burger 139
Honey Mustard Duck Confit
    Burger 141
Parmesan Duck Burger 137

EGGPLANT
Eggplant Parm Burger 109
Kofta Burger 75
Sun-Dried Tomato Chicken
    Burger 79
Sweet Potato Burger 121

EGGS
English Fry-Up Burger 83
Fish and Chips Burger 93
Mayo Tuna Burger 99
Spanish Tortilla Burger 131
Tonkatsu Burger 69
Zucchini Frittata Burger 127

ENDIVES
Maroilles and Endive Burger 47

ENGLISH MUFFINS
English Fry-Up Burger 83

FALAFEL
Falafel Burger 129

FETA CHEESE
Mint Feta Chicken Burger 81
Zucchini Frittata Burger 127

FOIE GRAS
Foie Gras Burger 135
Foie Gras and Duck Burger 139

FRIED FISH
Fish and Chips Burger 93
Tartar Fried Fish Burger 95

GOAT CHEESE
Pesto Grilled Veggies 107
Sun-Dried Tomato Chicken Burger 79

GOUDA CHEESE
Gouda Navy Bean Burger 119

GUACAMOLE
Guacamole Lentil Burger 125
Tex-Mex Burger 71

HAM
Laughing Cow and Ham Burger 55

HASH BROWNS
Tomme and Rösti Burger 43

HERB BUTTER
Mushroom Spinach Burger 111
Parmesan Duck Burger 137

HUMMUS
Falafel Burger 129
Hummus Beet Burger 113

JALAPEÑOS
Spicy Cheesesteak 17
Teriyaki Beef Burger 65

KETCHUP
Burger with Fried Onions and Pickles..........5

Cheeseburger.................................7
Double Cheeseburger 9
Hot Dog Burger 29

LEMON
Tzatziki Dill Salmon Burger 89

LENTILS
Guacamole Lentil Burger 125

LETTUCE, BUTTER
Fried Calamari Burger with Aioli 103
Onion Ring Burger 21
Spanish Tortilla Burger 131
Tartar Fried Fish Burger 95
Tomme and Rösti Burger 43

LETTUCE, FRISÉE
Cantal and Shallot Burger................. 31
Honey Mustard Duck Confit
    Burger 141

LETTUCE, ICEBERG
Chicken Nugget Burger 23
Tzatziki Dill Salmon Burger 89

LETTUCE, RED LEAF
Hawaiian Burger 63
Laughing Cow and Ham Burger 55
Sweet Potato Burger 121

LETTUCE, ROMAINE
Chicken BLT................................. 25
Chicken Caesar Burger 27

MÂCHE (LAMB'S LETTUCE)
Apple Camembert Burger 45
Mont d'Or and Sausage Burger 41
Parmesan Duck Burger 137
Raclette Burger 37

MANGO CHUTNEY
Pineapple Mango Chicken
    Burger 73

MAROILLES CHEESE
Maroilles and Endive Burger 47

MAYONNAISE
Avocado Salmon Burger 91
Banh Mi Burger 61
Chicken BLT................................. 25
Chicken Nugget Burger 23
Mayo Tuna Burger 99
Spanish Tortilla Burger 131
Surf and Turf Burger 85
Teriyaki Beef Burger 65

MINT
Mint Feta Chicken Burger 81
Zucchini Frittata Burger 127

MONT D'OR CHEESE
Mont d'Or and Sausage Burger 41

MOZZARELLA CHEESE
Eggplant Parm Burger 109
Mushroom Spinach Burger 111
Pesto Caprese Burger 77
Pizza Burger 15
Veggie Pesto Caprese Burger 115

MUENSTER CHEESE
Muenster and Sauerkraut Burger 49

MUSHROOMS
Beaufort and Mushroom Burger 33
Foie Gras Duck Burger 135
Mushroom Spinach Burger 111

MUSTARD
Burger with Fried Onions and Pickles..........5
Hot Dog Burger 29
Maroilles and Endive Burger 47
Mont d'Or and Sausage Burger 41
Muenster and Sauerkraut Burger 49

MUSTARD, WHOLE-GRAIN
Honey Mustard Duck Confit
    Burger 141
Mustard Beaufort Burger 51

ONIONS
Bacon Cheeseburger 11
Beaufort and Mushroom Burger............. 33
Cheeseburger.................................7
Cheese-Stuffed Burger 13
Chorizo Cod Burger 105
Eggplant Parm Burger 109
Falafel Burger 129
Foie Gras Burger 135
Honey Mustard Duck Confit
    Burger 141
Kofta Burger 75
Onion Ring Burger 21
Peppery Tomme and Chicken
    Burger 53
Pesto Grilled Veggies 107
Pulled Pork and Red Cabbage 19
Salmon Bagel...............................87
Spanish Tortilla Burger 131
Spicy Cheesesteak 17
Spinach and Blue Cheese Burger 35
Tartiflette Burger...........................39
Tex-Mex Burger 71

ONIONS, FRENCH FRIED
Burger with Fried Onions and Pickles..........5
Hot Dog Burger 29

PANCETTA
Tartiflette Burger...........................39

PARMESAN CHEESE
Chicken Caesar Burger 27
Parmesan Duck Burger 137

PARSLEY
Fried Calamari Burger with Aioli 103

PESTO
Pesto Caprese Burger 77
Pesto Grilled Veggies 107
Veggie Pesto Caprese Burger 115

PICCALILLI SAUCE
Piccalilli Veggie Burger 123

PICKLES
Burger with Fried Onions and Pickles..........5
Cheeseburger.................................7
Double Cheeseburger 9
Maroilles and Endive Burger 47
Raclette Burger 37
Tartar Fried Fish Burger 95

PINEAPPLE
Hawaiian Burger 63
Pineapple Mango Chicken
    Burger 73

PORK
Pulled Pork and Red Cabbage 19
Tonkatsu Burger...........................69

PORK SAUSAGE
Banh Mi Burger.................................. 61
English Fry-Up Burger 83
Hawaiian Burger 63
Mont d'Or and Sausage Burger 41
Surf and Turf Burger 85

POTATO CHIPS
Fish and Chips Burger............................. 93

POTATOES
Spanish Tortilla Burger........................131
Sweet Potato Burger...................121

RACLETTE CHEESE
Raclette Burger 37

REBLOCHON CHEESE
Tartiflette Burger.................................39

ROQUEFORT CHEESE
Spinach and Blue Cheese Burger 35

SALMON
Avocado Salmon Burger 91
Salmon Bagel...............................87
Tzatziki Dill Salmon Burger 89

SAUERKRAUT
Muenster and Sauerkraut Burger...........49

SCALLIONS
Mayo Tuna Burger 99
Shrimp Meze Burger......................101
Tzatziki Chickpea Burger.......................117
Yakitori Chicken Burger.......................67

SHALLOTS
Cantal and Shallot Burger........................ 31

SHRIMP
Shrimp Meze Burger...........................101
Surf and Turf Burger 85

SOY SAUCE
Avocado Salmon Burger 91
Soy Tofu Burger 133

SPECIAL SAUCE
Cheese-Stuffed Burger 13
Chorizo Cod Burger 105
Gouda Navy Bean Burger.....................119
Laughing Cow and Ham Burger 55
Tomme and Rösti Burger 43

SPINACH
Foie Gras and Duck Burger....................139
Mushroom Spinach Burger......................111
Mustard Beaufort Burger..................... 51
Spinach and Blue Cheese Burger 35

SWEET POTATO
Sweet Potato Burger.......................121

TARAMOSALATA
Shrimp Meze Burger.........................101

TARTAR SAUCE
Raclette Burger 37
Tartar Fried Fish Burger 95

TERIYAKI SAUCE
Teriyaki Beef Burger 65
Yakitori Chicken Burger.......................67

TOFU
Soy Tofu Burger 133

TOMATOES
Cheese-Stuffed Burger 13
Chicken BLT....................................... 25
Chicken Nugget Burger.....................23
Falafel Burger.................................129
Gouda Navy Bean Burger.....................119
Hummus Beet Burger...........................113
Mayo Tuna Burger 99
Mint Feta Chicken Burger.................. 81

Onion Ring Burger 21
Piccalilli Veggie Burger 123
Tzatziki Chickpea Burger.......................117
Veggie Pesto Caprese Burger 115

TOMATOES, SUN-DRIED
Pesto Caprese Burger 77
Sun-Dried Tomato Chicken
  Burger...79

TOMATO SAUCE/PUREE
Eggplant Parm Burger 109
Pizza Burger.................................... 15

TOMME CHEESE
Peppery Tomme and Chicken
  Burger.. 53
Tomme and Rösti Burger 43

TUNA
Mayo Tuna Burger 99

TZATZIKI
Chicken Tikka Burger...........................57
Mint Feta Chicken Burger..................... 81
Tzatziki Chickpea Burger.......................117
Tzatziki Dill Salmon Burger 89

VINEGAR
Banh Mi Burger............................ 61
Cantal and Shallot Burger.................... 31
Fish and Chips Burger.................. 93
Foie Gras Burger.............................135

YOGURT, GREEK
Foie Gras and Duck Burger.................... 139
Mustard Beaufort Burger..................... 51
Spinach and Blue Cheese Burger 35

ZUCCHINI
Soy Tofu Burger 133
Zucchini Frittata Burger...........................127

Translation copyright © 2018 by Hachette Livre (Marabout)

Photographs copyright © 2018 by Charlotte Lascève

All rights reserved.

Published in the United States by Clarkson Potter/Publishers, an imprint of the Crown Publishing Group, a division of Penguin Random House LLC, New York. Originally published in France as *Burger Super Facile* by Marabout, a division of Hachette Livre, Paris, 2017. Copyright © 2017 by Hachette Livre (Marabout).

crownpublishing.com

clarksonpotter.com

CLARKSON POTTER is a trademark and POTTER with colophon is a registered trademark of Penguin Random House LLC.

Library of Congress Cataloging-in-Publication Data

Names: Souksisavanh, Orathay, author. | Translation of: Souksisavanh, Orathay. Burger super facile.

Title: Super easy burgers : 69 really simple recipes / Orathay Souksisavanh.

Other titles: Burger super facile. English

Description: First edition. | New York : Clarkson Potter/Publishers, 2018. | Includes index.

Identifiers: LCCN 2017030823 (print) | LCCN 2017031068 (ebook) | ISBN 9780525572978 (Ebook) | ISBN 9780525572961 (trade pbk.)

Subjects: LCSH: Sandwiches. | Hamburgers. | Quick and easy cooking. | LCGFT: Cookbooks.

Classification: LCC TX818 (ebook) | LCC TX818 .S62913 2018 (print) | DDC 641.84--dc23

LC record available at https://lccn.loc.gov/2017030823

ISBN 978-0-525-57296-1

Ebook ISBN 978-0-525-57297-8

Printed in China

Translation by Nicholas LoVecchio

10 9 8 7 6 5 4 3 2 1

First American Edition